Outsiders!

Written by Kerrie Shanahan

Illustrated by Walter Carzon

Flying Start
to Literacy®

Contents

Preface

This is a fictional story about an imaginary uncontacted tribe, and what might happen if "outsiders" were heading towards their home.

Uncontacted people are groups of people who have no contact with the outside world. They live in remote places that are difficult to get to.

We don't know a lot about these people or how they live. We do know they have their own cultures and traditions, and that they don't need modern technology to meet their needs.

We know that most of these groups are afraid of contact with outside people. There is a long history of outsiders attacking and killing remote tribes, and taking their land so they can log trees, mine for gold or build farms.

Another reason for their fear is that uncontacted people have no immunity to diseases such as measles, the flu or common colds. These illnesses spread quickly through uncontacted tribes and can kill many people.

So what might uncontacted people do if outsiders confronted them?

Chapter 1

A close call

"Listen, Maya!" Jumi's voice was low and urgent.

Maya froze. All her senses were heightened.
She scanned the thick jungle. Then she heard the
sound . . . footsteps! They were distant but heading
their way.

"Run!" she hissed back.

The two friends fled. They sprinted out of the clearing
and into the jungle. They ran lightly across the forest
floor, ducking and weaving under branches and around
vine-covered trees. Finally, they stopped behind a tall,
wide tree. They crouched down, desperately trying to
catch their breath.

"Can you see anyone?" Maya whispered.

Jumi peered around the tree trunk. He inhaled sharply
as he caught sight of them . . . Outsiders!

"Look!" Jumi was instantly filled with both fear and excitement.

Maya's mouth dropped open as she, too, saw the group of strangely-dressed men walking through their jungle.

"We have to get out of here!" Maya knew outsiders were dangerous – they could attack her tribe and destroy her village.

Maya and Jumi had grown up being warned about outsiders. They knew the stories about tribes that had their villages taken away by outsiders. And they knew about members of tribes who got sick and died after letting outsiders stay in their villages.

"Come on, Jumi!" Maya was anxious to get away from the danger.

"Wait," Jumi whispered. He was fascinated to see outsiders in their forest. He couldn't take his eyes off them.

"Well, I'm getting out of here." Maya's voice was urgent.

She took off, and Jumi reluctantly followed.

They reached the stream, and Maya flew across the log bridge with Jumi close behind her. They moved through the jungle with ease. This was their place – their backyard.

They dashed along until they were far enough away for Maya to feel safe. Then they walked side by side in silence. It was a long walk. They both loved exploring, but they hadn't realised they had wandered so far from their village. And they had not expected to see outsiders!

Chapter 2
Questions

Jumi knew outsiders could be dangerous, but he was also curious about them and his mind filled with questions. *What are they doing here? Are they friendly? Where do they live?* Secretly, he sometimes wondered if he might leave the village one day and explore faraway places.

The friends were close to home when Jumi voiced his thoughts. "It would be amazing to meet those outsiders we saw!"

"Jumi!" Maya said sharply. "Those outsiders could kill us! Don't start talking about outsiders, and leaving, and seeking adventure. You know what happened to Uncle Tavan. He left and never came back!"

"Okay, okay," Jumi backtracked. "I'm just curious."

"Good," said Maya. "Now, let's get back and tell the elders what we saw."

"No," Jumi said firmly. "Please don't tell. Not yet."

Maya's dark eyes grew wide. "We have to tell. We could be in danger."

"I just want the chance to see them again. From a distance," Jumi pleaded. "If we tell the elders, we'll never be allowed to leave the village."

Maya wasn't sure. Her instincts urged her to tell. The tribe needed to know. And the neighbouring tribes should be told, too. These outsiders might want all of their land.

But she also knew the encounter meant a lot to Jumi. And maybe if he got to see the outsiders again, he would stop thinking about leaving home. Maya wasn't sure what to do.

Maya sighed. "Okay. I won't tell."

Jumi was her best friend. She wanted him to be happy. But her stomach churned and her mind raced. What had she agreed to?

"Thank you," said Jumi with relief. He hoped to see the outsiders again. And he wondered . . . *If they are friendly, maybe I can leave with them and see some new places.*

"But Jumi," Maya said, "if we see them a second time, we definitely must tell the elders. Agree?"

"Agree!"

The next day, Maya and Jumi went about their normal chores – tending the garden, collecting wood and fresh water, and gathering fruits and berries. Then they had their lessons with the elders, during which they learnt about the language and culture of their people.

In the evening, they headed off on the well-worn track out of the village. They reached a clearing and scanned the hills, trying to spot any outsiders.

"No sign of anyone," Maya announced.

"I guess they've gone." Jumi was disappointed.

"And now, it doesn't matter that we didn't tell about seeing those people," said Maya.

But deep down, she wasn't sure. What if the outsiders were still lurking in the jungle? Should she and Jumi really be keeping such a big secret when there was so much at risk?

Chapter 3
Celebration Day

Maya awoke the next day with all thoughts of outsiders gone. It was Celebration Day!

She skipped out of her family's hut, but stopped when she saw her mother. Celebration Day was a bittersweet time for Maya's mother.

"Uncle Tavan?" Maya asked her, knowing the answer.

Maya's mum nodded.

"I miss him, too, Mum."

Maya would never forget that Celebration Day, many years ago. She had been young, but the memory was etched in her mind. Like always, it had been a wonderful day – delicious food, singing, dancing and stories.

But then Maya's uncle Tavan told everyone he was leaving. He wanted to leave the jungle and experience what was outside their small village. He was only 17 at the time.

Uncle Tavan promised that he wouldn't leave forever, that he would come back, but that didn't stop the sobbing and the desperate protests from members of his family. He hugged everyone and walked out of the jungle.

So far, Uncle Tavan had not returned. Most people didn't expect him to. And many people worried that more of their people would leave like Uncle Tavan did. How would the tribe survive if all the young people left?

"Come on." Maya's mum tried hard to be cheerful. "We've got lots to do."

Maya and her mum and the other women began getting the food for the feast ready – preparing meat and fish to be cooked, and arranging platters of fruits, berries and nuts.

The village was abuzz. People were cleaning their huts, getting the campfires ready, and organising masks and body paint for the dancing and storytelling. Everyone was busy, and all the activity was laced with anticipation.

It wasn't often that all fifty-plus members of their village gathered. Groups of men were regularly away on hunting expeditions, or staying at the seasonal fishing villages along the river. And sometimes, scouting groups were away for days, checking for signs of outsiders or meeting with other villagers.

But everyone was present for Celebration Day.

In the middle of the hot day, everyone in the village rested. Jumi and Maya decided to have a quick swim in the stream. But halfway there, Maya stopped dead in her tracks. She pointed across the valley, where she could see figures moving among the trees.

"Outsiders!" she shrieked. "This time we have to tell!"

Maya and Jumi turned and sprinted back along the track.

"Outsiders! Outsiders!" they yelled as they dashed into the village courtyard. "Lots of them! Coming our way!"

Chapter 4
A tribe in trouble

Their warning spread rapidly through the village. Some men grabbed weapons – arrows, axes and spears. One shouted, "We must defend our home!" They wanted to attack the outsiders.

"No!" said the elders. "Maya said there are lots of them. We would have no chance against such a large group with their deadly, exploding weapons. We must leave. Now!"

Panic set in. Parents gathered up their children and took off into the jungle. They scattered in all directions. The evacuation looked chaotic and random, but it was preplanned. If outsiders came close to their village, they knew to run in different directions. It was much easier to hide in smaller family groups than to hide together as one big group.

Maya and the others in her family hurried through the jungle until they were a fair distance from the village. They huddled together quietly and waited.

Hours passed. They had not seen or heard another soul. Maybe the outsiders had gone. Maybe the villagers were safe. They couldn't be sure. They waited until dusk turned into night. Then they slowly and carefully began to trek to the pre-arranged meeting spot in another part of the jungle.

The next morning, everyone was relieved that all 54 villagers had made it safely to their meeting place. The elders met and formulated a plan.

They announced that five scouts would track down the outsiders and follow them.

"Matis will lead the expedition," the elders explained. "We must be certain that they are not in our village. We also need to know where these outsiders are and what they are doing in our jungle."

"Maya, your dad is leading the tracking group," Jumi said. He was excited. And he had an idea. "We should go, too. We could show them where we first saw the outsiders. That could be really helpful."

Maya stared at Jumi. "Are you serious? We can't tell. We'll get into so much trouble."

But Jumi had made up his mind. "We must! And I'll ask if we can go with your dad." Jumi was also thinking that this could be his only chance to meet the outsiders.

Jumi marched over to the elders, and his story spilled out in one long speech.

"So that's why Maya and I should go with the expedition. We can help!"

He stopped and looked up at the elders. They looked back with anger in their eyes, but they didn't have time for that. They turned and huddled together in deep discussion.

21

"You can go!" one of the elders announced. "But," he added sternly, "you must listen to Matis and do exactly what he says."

Maya and Jumi nodded. They joined Matis and the other trackers, and they all flitted silently through the jungle. They made quick time getting back to their village. It was empty and untouched.

"Good," said Matis. "Our village is safe. Everyone can come back home." He then sent two of the trackers back to relay this good news to the rest of their people.

"Okay, you two," Matis nodded to Maya and Jumi. "You take the lead now. Show us where you saw the outsiders."

Jumi and Maya lost no time in leading them towards the clearing where they first saw the outsiders.

They were almost there when Maya suddenly stopped. She crouched down and pointed to marks in the forest floor. Matis looked, too. He nodded. Fresh shoe prints. "Good job, Maya," he said.

Matis took the lead again, following the prints through the dense jungle. They soon caught up to the humans leaving the prints – the outsiders!

Matis and his group were careful to stay a safe distance behind. After hours of trekking through the jungle, the outsiders stopped at the banks of the big river. They sat in small groups and spoke in muted voices.

Matis, Maya, Jumi and the other trackers watched the outsiders silently from afar. What were they doing? What were they waiting for? Were they planning an attack?

Chapter 5

An unexpected meeting

"*Taaaaa- Whoooo!*" It was the call the villagers used to gain one another's attention. Maya, Jumi and Matis were confused. Who was calling them? They quietly crept in the direction of the sound, and they could not believe who they saw standing in the middle of a small clearing.

"Uncle Tavan?" Maya stared in disbelief.

"Maya, you're so big now." Uncle Tavan smiled at his niece.

Maya instinctively tried to run to Uncle Tavan, but Matis grabbed her arm.

"Wait!" he ordered.

"Yes, stop, Maya!" warned Uncle Tavan. "Do not come close."

"What are you doing here?" Matis called sternly. He was unsure how to treat this man who had upset his family so much when he left suddenly all those years ago.

"I'm helping the outsiders you are watching," Uncle Tavan explained. "I'm sorry I scared you by bringing them here, but it's so they can keep dangerous outsiders away. They want to help."

Matis sighed with relief. He had been so worried that these strangers were here to destroy their village and take their land.

"You made us so sad when you left us, Uncle Tavan."
Tears ran down Maya's cheeks.

"I'm sorry I upset you, but I had to go. I wanted to see more of the world." Uncle Tavan fought back tears as he spoke. "I miss everyone, too. I saw the village all set up for Celebration Day. It made me sad to see everything I love left behind."

"But please tell everyone that I am happy," Uncle Tavan continued, smiling through his unshed tears. "I have a lovely family. A wife and two small boys."

"New cousins!" Maya beamed. "Can you bring them to the village?"

"I can't. If I did, I could bring diseases to the village." Tavan's voice was shaky. "The diseases I've been exposed to in the outside world could kill you. I can never return."

Maya and the others stared at Uncle Tavan as they processed this news.

"I must go." Uncle Tavan knew he had been absent from his group long enough. "We are leaving on a big boat, and it will be here any minute."

"Wait, Uncle Tavan!" said Jumi. "What is it like in the world of the outsiders?"

"There are good and bad parts. But remember, if you leave the village, you leave for good." And with that, Uncle Tavan turned and took off into the thick jungle.

Maya, Jumi and Matis stood in stunned silence.

"It's time for us to go back to the village," said Matis at last. "We have lots of news."

Chapter 6
Safe again

When the tired group of trackers arrived back at the village, they were greeted like heroes. They excitedly relayed the news about Uncle Tavan, as well as his messages. And when Matis explained that the outsiders were leaving on the big boat, everyone cheered. Their village was safe again.

Maya's mum was so glad to hear that Uncle Tavan was healthy and happy, and Maya wanted to tell her everything about their meeting. But that had to wait because the elders were motioning for her and Jumi to join them.

"Well done," one of the elders began. "Matis said your help was invaluable."

Maya beamed with pride, and Jumi sighed with relief.

"But there's still the matter of keeping your first sighting of the outsiders a secret," another elder said. The elders hadn't finished with them yet. "That secret could have destroyed our village. You put us all in terrible danger."

"Sorry." Maya and Jumi bowed their heads.

"Because of your bad decision, you must spend extra time teaching our younger children about the jungle and how to be safe in it. Now, go and see your families and get some rest."

Maya and Jumi knew the elders had gone easy on them – they had gotten off lightly!

A week later, Maya found Jumi and signalled for him to follow her into the jungle. After some time, Maya stopped and pulled something out from under some fallen leaves.

"I found this." She handed a small crumpled notebook to Jumi. "The outsiders left it behind. You can have it. I know you're interested in all that outsider stuff."

Jumi's mouth dropped open. He gently stroked the paper. "Wow." He was stunned. He had never seen such a thing. He turned it over in his hands and opened the book, turning the pages one by one. "Look at these drawings and strange markings," he said breathlessly. "Thanks, Maya!"

"I don't want you to ever, ever leave us," Maya said seriously. "Look what happened to Uncle Tavan. He can never come back."

"I know." Jumi was thoughtful. "After listening to Uncle Tavan, I've decided I'll never leave by myself. But if you come with me . . ."

"Well, that will never happen!" Maya wanted this conversation to end.

We'll see . . . Jumi said to himself.

Then the two friends made their way back home, through the jungle . . . *their* jungle.

A note from the author

As I wrote this story, I thought about a time in my life when I left home to live in a big city. My memories of this time helped me to imagine the feelings that Jumi might have when he thought about leaving his home – a mixture of excitement and fear!

To write this story, I used information about how remote tribes live. I also had to "fill in the gaps" by imagining what it might be like for kids growing up in an uncontacted tribe. What might they think about the rest of us? Would they fear outsiders? Or would they want to leave their tribe to find out more about them? Of course not everyone would have the same opinion, and that's what I wanted to show through the characters of Jumi and Maya.

I hope you enjoyed their adventure!